THE TWELVE GIFTS OF JESUS

Twelve Divine Gifts That Change Everything

Pastor Paul Steven Smith

KG
KAMB
PUBLISHING
GROUP

Kamb Publishing Group

Printed in the United States of America First Edition, 2025

For more books, sermons, and creative works by Pastor Paul Steven Smith, visit:

www.paulstevensmith.com

Dedication

A Christmas Dedication—The Holy Ghost Holiday Edition

This book is dedicated to everybody who made it through this year by the grace of God, peppermint tea, and pure determination.

This is for those who had a "Silent Night," not because it was peaceful, but because you were too tired to argue.

To the folks who said, "Lord, if these people do not act right at this Christmas dinner, I'm about to lay hands—and not in the biblical way," may the peace of Jesus be upon you EXTRA strong.

To anyone who tried to recreate the joy from a Hallmark Christmas movie but ended up with burnt cookies, missing receipts, and relatives who overstay—I see you. I love you. This book will bless you.

To the grown folks still healing from childhood Christmas trauma—like not getting the toy you prayed for, or someone giving you socks again like you weren't believing God for a bike—may this year's gifts be spiritual and satisfying.

To the families who celebrate with empty chairs—may laughter still find you. To the ones celebrating alone—may Jesus Himself sit on your couch and keep you company. (Do not offer Him fruitcake. Nobody likes that.)

I dedicate this book with joy to the folks who love Christmas music only until December 26th—after that, Mariah Carey must return to her winter cave.

And finally—to JESUS:

The real reason we got hope, strength, peace, and grace... and the only reason some of us didn't lose our minds in 2025.

Thank You for being the ultimate Christmas Gift, even though You arrived with no wrapping paper, no bow, and no Amazon tracking number.

Merry Christmas, everybody. Unwrap these gifts like they're the good kind—not the kind your auntie bought on sale.

— *Pastor Paul*

Epigraph

"Heaven's greatest gift didn't sparkle, jingle, or shine. He breathed...and the world changed forever."

— Pastor Paul

Acknowledgments

I want to thank everyone who prayed for me, pushed me, corrected me, challenged me, and reminded me that I still have work to do.

To my Victory Fellowship Church family—you are my heartbeat. You keep me laughing, praying, growing, and believing.

Thank you to every friend who believed in my calling when I doubted myself—you saw Pastor Paul when all I could see was Paul.

To those who accompanied me through my challenges, you served as a pillar of strength when my own hands faltered.

And finally, to every reader who has ever carried pain, fear, confusion, or hope inside their soul—thank you for letting me speak into your life. May these twelve gifts bless you the way Jesus blessed me.

Preface

Why These Gifts Matter

Before you flip through the pages, let me be clear:

This publication is not a Christmas storybook.

This is a survival manual wrapped in holiday lights.

These twelve gifts are not ornaments—they are weapons, medicine, healing, identity, strength, and revelation. They are the gifts Jesus keeps giving long after December is over.

As I wrote this book, I realized something powerful:

Every one of these gifts saved me at a different time in my life. And if Jesus gave them to me, He will give them to you.

So, take your time. Breathe through every chapter. Highlight. Cry. Laugh. Holler "MY LORD!" if you need to. This book is not meant to be read—it's meant to be experienced.

Let's unwrap these gifts together.

A Note To The Reader

Beloved,

Read this book with expectation. Please read it with openness. Read it with the belief that God has something for you on these pages.

This book is a journey. A celebration. A conversation between your soul and your Savior. You may feel something shift inside you.

You may feel something break free. You may feel something restore itself.

Good. That means the gifts are working.

And remember—Jesus didn't wrap these gifts for perfect people. He wrapped them for REAL people. People like me. People like you.

People who are still learning, still healing, still growing, still believing, and still showing up.

Welcome to The Twelve Gifts of Jesus.

Let's begin.

Foreword

When you meet Pastor Paul Steven Smith, you do not just hear his words — you feel them.

He has a way of talking that reaches past your ears and grabs your heart by the collar. He blends revelation with humor, wisdom with real-life grit, and the Holy Ghost with a little "don't play with me" attitude.

For years, I watched Pastor Paul pour into people who were hanging on by a thread — and somehow, he turned those threads into ropes that pulled them out of darkness.

This book is no different.

The Twelve Gifts of Jesus is more than a Christmas book. It's a spiritual survival kit. A winter coat for the soul. A prophetic reminder that you are loved, valued, chosen, and covered.

Pastor Paul wrote these chapters with honesty, fire, and tenderness. If you let these words work on you, the same Jesus who healed him, lifted him, strengthened him, and carried him will do the same for you.

So, sit back. Take a breath. Prepare your heart.

You're not just opening a book—you're unwrapping heaven's gifts.

— *A Friend Who Has Sat Under His Voice and Walked Away Changed*

Bishop Vandy Kennedy, Walker Mill Baptist Church, Capitol Heights, Maryland

Christmas Blessing

From My Heart to Yours

Before you dive into these gifts, before you turn the next page, before December sweeps you up in lights, lists, and leftovers — I want to speak a blessing over you and your whole household.

Because listen... Christmas hits everybody differently.

Some folks are out here jingling bells like extras in a Hallmark movie. Some folks are holding it together with peppermint and prayer. And some of us... well, we're just trying to survive these family gatherings without saying the wrong thing to the wrong cousin or catching a case.

But regardless of where you fall in that mix, I want you to know this:

You are loved. You are seen. You are carried. You are covered. And you are not going into this season alone. May your home be full of laughter—the loud kind that makes people look at you funny in public places.

May your tears be holy—the kind that wash old wounds and make room for joy to return.

May your memories be sweet, and your grief be gentle, and your hope be stubborn enough to rise even when your heart feels tired.

May you find time to breathe—deep, slow, healing breaths—because Christmas is not a performance. It is a reminder that God stepped into our mess so we would never face it without Him.

And Lord... for the families gathering this year:

Bless the ones cooking in the kitchen, the ones hiding from drama in the basement, and the ones sneaking extra slices of pie when nobody's watching.

Bless Auntie Who Talks Too Loud, Cousin Who Brings Nothing But Leaves With Everything, and Uncle Who Always Starts The Same Story Every Year At Exactly 4:17 pm.

Bless the ones who showed up cheerful... and bless the ones who showed up broken but didn't know how to say it.

Bless the ones who are missing loved ones at the table this year. Wrap them tight in peace that does not ask them to "be strong" but lets them feel and heal at their own pace.

Bless the ones celebrating alone—may laughter find them, may comfort surround them, and may joy knock on their door unexpectedly.

Most of all...

May the love of Jesus slip into your home, sit on your couch, slide into your spirit, and settle in your heart like warm cocoa on a cold night.

Because the greatest gift of Christmas isn't found under your tree.

It's found right where you are... breathing through you, carrying you, holding you up even when you feel like folding. Merry Christmas, my friend. May these gifts change your life—because you deserve a season full of miracles.

— *Pastor Paul*

Christmas Blessing
Prayer

Dear Jesus,

As we open these pages, open our hearts.

As we unwrap these gifts, unwrap the places inside us that have been hidden, hurting, or hardened. Let Your grace fall like fresh snow.

Let Your peace settle like a quiet night.

Let Your love shine like a star over Bethlehem. Bless the one reading this.

Bless their home. Bless their mind. Bless their family. Bless their past, present, and future.

May every chapter bring healing. May every gift bring revelation.

May every page remind them that You are still Emmanuel—God with us, God for us, God in us.

In Jesus' name, amen.

Contents

Introduction

The Gift Before the Gifts

L et me start by telling you something real:

Most of us grow up thinking Christmas is about the gifts under the tree. But the older I got, the more I realized the real gifts are the ones God places inside us.

Gifts wrapped in: Grace, Mercy, Strength, Calling, Purpose, Healing, Identity, Hope, Peace, Salvation.

Those are the gifts that don't fade, don't break, don't expire, and don't need batteries. Every chapter you're about to read is a reminder that Jesus didn't just come TO the world—HE came FOR you.

He came to restore every part of you that life tried to steal. He came to give you gifts you didn't even know you needed. He came to pull you out of fear and push you into freedom.

This book is your Christmas morning for the soul. Let's open the first gift.

Gift Number One

The Gift of Presence

On the first day of Christmas, Jesus gave to me...
The Gift of Presence (so I never have to walk alone).

When Jesus Steps In, Emptiness Steps Out

Some gifts do not fit under a tree. Some gifts do not come wrapped in red paper with shiny bows. There are some gifts so divine, so necessary, so life-saving that heaven said, "This one must be given first."

And the first gift Jesus gives you is not a blessing... not a miracle... not a breakthrough... but Himself. His presence. His nearness. His here-ness.

Because sometimes the greatest gift you will ever receive is not being alone anymore.

The Gift of Presence is not just "God with us" from a Christmas storybook. It is "God with YOU" in the mess, in the storm, in the confusion, in the waiting room, in the heartbreak, and in the moments where your soul is shivering and your spirit feels like an unplugged lamp. This is the gift where Jesus steps into the room before explanation shows up, before answers arrive, before clarity makes sense—and He stands there like, "Yeah, I see the chaos. I see the fear. I see what you're fighting. But I am here. And My presence changes everything."

The Gift That Walks In When Everybody Else Walks Out

People show up for the celebration but disappear during the suffering. They love you when the lights are on, when the laughter is loud, when you are winning, and when you are shining. But let trouble tap your shoulder... let life flip a table on you... let disappointment break into your week like a thief... And suddenly the room gets real empty, real fast.

But Jesus? He is built differently. He does not wait for an invitation. He walks into your storm like He owns the weather. He shows up in your sadness like He has the key to your healing. He stands in your dark like a flame that cannot be blown out.

I remember one Christmas Eve sitting in a room full of people laughing, yet feeling completely invisible. I was surrounded by noise but drowning in silence. That is exactly when His Presence sat down next to me and whispered, "I see you." His presence does not flinch, fold, or flee. That is why this is Gift Number One. Because if all you receive this year is His presence, you already have enough.

The Presence That Feels You Even When You Do Not Feel Him

You will not always feel God. Feelings are cute. Feelings can fool you. Feelings change their mind every fifteen seconds. But presence is steady. Presence is faithful. Presence is committed. Presence says, "I am not going anywhere."

Sometimes you will wonder, "Lord... are You even here?" And He will whisper back, "I never left."

Sometimes His presence hides long enough for your faith to strengthen. Sometimes His presence gets quiet because He is working beneath the surface. Sometimes His presence steps back so you can step up.

Silence is not absence—silence is strategy. And even when you cannot feel Him, He is holding your whole world together with His bare hands.

The Gift That Protects You When You Do Not See the Danger

You survived things you never even knew were trying to take you out because His presence intercepted the hit. You thought it was a coincidence. You thought it was luck. You thought it was a close call. No—that was presence.

Jesus stood in front of something you never saw coming. Jesus blocked a trap that had your name on it. Jesus shut a door that looked good but would have destroyed you. Jesus whispered, "Not this one, not today," when the enemy sent nonsense your way.

His presence is not just comforting—it is covering.

You were kept. You were protected. You were carried. You were shielded. Because His presence never clocks out.

The Presence That Calls You Out of Your Fog

Have you ever been lost in your own head? Looping. Obsessing. Spiral-thinking. Creating a whole season of stress from one small situation? The Gift of Presence does not babysit your anxiety—it confronts it.

Jesus steps into your mental storm like, "No. This is not your reality. This is not your identity. This is not your truth.

Get up. Come out. Walk with Me."

His presence breaks illusions. His presence exposes lies. His presence wakes you up.

Some storms did not disappear—you just finally saw the storm-maker. And once His presence reveals it, you cannot unsee it. You grow, you shift, you evolve, and you stop falling for the same spiritual traps.

Presence matures you. Presence sharpens you. Presence grows you up.

The Gift That Sits With You in the Dark

Jesus knows how to sit with you in silence—not fixing you, not lecturing you, not pushing you, not preaching you into exhaustion. Just... sitting.

Some days, the most spiritual thing Jesus does is not leave.

His presence sits beside your grief and does not get uncomfortable. His presence sits beside your questions and does not get insecure. His presence sits beside your brokenness, saying, "Take your time. I am here."

There is healing in that kind of presence. There is strength in that kind of companionship. There is peace in knowing Jesus is not scared of your shadows.

This gift can carry you through December, through storms, through losses, through fear, through everything.

The Presence That Makes You Walk Differently

When you start living a presence-aware life, everything changes. Your posture straightens. Your decisions sharpen. Your confidence rises. Your peace deepens. Your boundaries strengthen.

Because you stop walking like a victim and start walking like someone escorted by heaven, you, plus His presence, are a problem for darkness.

Hell trembles when you wake up. Fear panics when you pray. Your past loses its grip. Your future gains momentum.

Not because you are strong—but because His presence makes you unshakeable.

Your Christmas Practice
Invite the Presence Daily

Don't just read this and move on. Do this today: Set a recurring alarm on your phone for 12:00 pm and label it "He Is Here." When it goes off—whether you are driving, cooking, or hiding in the bathroom—stop for ten seconds and whisper, "Jesus, I acknowledge You. Be here with me." Invite Him into the mundane. Invite Him into the mess. Invite Him into the miracle. Because the greatest gift you will unwrap this Christmas is not under a tree; it is found in your spirit. Jesus. Here. With you. Always.

This is Gift Number One: The Gift of Presence.

Gift Number Two
The Gift of Peace

On the second day of Christmas, Jesus gave to me...The Gift of Peace (because the storm outside can't touch the calm inside).

When Heaven Breathes, Storms Lose Their Voice

Some gifts sparkle, gifts that shine, gifts that make you smile... And then some gifts save your sanity.

Peace is that gift.

Not the quiet-in-the-room peace. Not the nobody's calling my phone, peace. Not the I-finally-paid-that-bill-on-time peace.

Oh no. This is the peace that walks into your spirit like a bouncer at a nightclub and throws out anything that does not belong.

Anxiety? Out. Fear? Out. Overthinking? Out. Stress? Out faster than a cousin who borrowed money and forgot their cashapp.

You see, we often get it twisted. We think peace is a feeling, like happiness or excitement. But let me correct that theology right now: Peace is not an emotion. Peace is not a mood. Peace is not the absence of conflict.

Peace is heaven, taking a deep breath inside your chest. Peace is Jesus drawing a circle around your soul and saying, "Nothing gets in unless I approve it." Peace is the supernatural quiet that does not match your natural chaos.

This is the second gift Jesus gives—Not because life gets easier, but because you get steadier.

The Peace That Makes No Sense—And Still Works

Let's be honest: human peace is cute... until life sneezes.

Human peace dissolves in traffic, melts under pressure, and evaporates the minute your boss sends that "We need to talk" email.

But Jesus gives you a peace that does not negotiate with circumstances. It sits. It stays. It settles. It refuses to be moved.

Heaven's peace laughs at storms. Heaven's peace ignores confusion. Heaven's peace stays calm even when you're two seconds from flipping a table like Jesus in the temple.

This is why Scripture says He gives a peace that "passes all understanding."

Meaning: You will not get it. People around you will not get it. Your situation won't match it. And your mind will be like, "Why am I not crying right now?"

Because Jesus loaned you His calm, and His calm cannot be broken.

The Gift of Peace Does Not Remove Your Storm—It Rebukes the Chaos Inside It

Let me tell you something real: Jesus never promised you a storm-free life. He promised you storm-proof peace.

That night on the boat, the disciples panicked like drama queens. They were shaking Jesus, yelling, "Master, do You not care that we are about to DIE?"

Meanwhile, Jesus was knocked out, as if he had a weighted blanket and a white-noise machine. Why? Because peace is not aware of panic—panic is aware of peace.

Jesus woke up, stretched like a man whose soul was fully rested, and said three simple words: "Peace. Be still." He did NOT say, "Storm, stop forever." "Disciples, stop overreacting." "Waves, calm down for good."

He spoke to the spirit of chaos—not the weather.

That is what the Gift of Peace does for you. It speaks to the chaos in your thoughts, emotions, expectations, fears, assumptions, memories, and wounds. And it commands, "Be still. You do not run this house."

The Peace That Teaches You How to Breathe Again

Some people breathe air. Some of us? We breathe anxiety until Jesus intervenes.

Peace teaches you how to breathe without fear, breathe without rushing, breathe without apologizing, breathe without bracing for impact, and breathe without pretending.

Peace slows your soul down until it remembers what rest feels like.

Peace unclenches your jaw. Peace drops your shoulders. Peace stops your mind from running marathons at 3 am.

Peace turns the volume down in rooms that used to shout at you.

This is not holiday peace—this is holy peace. Peace that reaches into your rib cage and releases you from battles you no longer need to fight.

The Peace That Protects Your Mental Health

Let me tell you something folks won't admit openly: Most of us have been one bad day away from shutting down completely.

I've been there. I remember staring at a ceiling fan at 2:00 am, my mind racing through every possible "what if" scenario. But then, I felt it. A quiet settling. It didn't make sense, but it made me sleep. That was the Gift of Peace guarding my mind.

The Gift of Peace is God's way of saying, "I refuse to let your mind collapse under the weight I never asked you to carry."

Peace guards your thoughts like a security officer with a clipboard: "Stress? Not on the list. Overthinking? Try again. Fear? Nope. Depression? You are not authorized to enter."

Peace is not passive—Peace is PROTECTIVE.

It steps between you and whatever tries to hijack your mind.

Jesus' peace is spiritual therapy without a co-pay. It heals. It steadies. It clears the clutter. It dismantles lies. It brings light into corners you have been afraid to face.

That is why His peace is a GIFT... Because you could not create it yourself even if you tried.

The Peace That Makes People Ask, "How Are You Still Standing?"

If you have lived long enough, you know this truth: You will go through things that should have shattered you.

And yet... You are still standing. Still smiling. Still breathing. Still moving. Still pushing. Still growing. Still believing. Still surviving what tried to bury you.

People think it's a strength. But it is peace. Supernatural peace that kept your mind from breaking.

Peace held you together when life tried to scatter you. Peace kept you grounded when circumstances tried to uproot you. Peace walked with you into rooms you were afraid of. Peace whispered, "I got you," when your heart whispered back, "I don't know if I can do this."

Peace is the quiet miracle you have been living in without realizing it.

The Peace That Sets You Free From Every "What If."

"What if this goes wrong?" "What if they leave?" "What if I fail?" "What if I cannot recover?" "What if I am not enough?"

Whew. The "what ifs" will drain your soul if you let them. But the Gift of Peace cuts the cord.

Peace says, "What if God provides?" "What if God strengthens you?" "What if God surprises you?" "What if God restores you?" "What if God already handled it?"

Peace replaces fear-filled imagination with faith-filled expectancy. You stop rehearsing disaster. And start expecting glory.

Your Christmas Peace Practice
A Simple Prayer

This week, catch yourself spiraling. When your thoughts speed up, stop. Put your hand on your chest, take a deep breath, and say out loud, "Jesus, breathe Your peace into me right now." Do not rush it. Wait until you feel your shoulders drop. Invite Him. Welcome Him. Let Him settle your soul like fresh snow settling on a quiet street. Because the second gift of Jesus—the peace that calms storms, stills hearts, and strengthens minds—is already yours.

This is Gift Number Two: The Gift of Peace.

Gift Number Three
The Gift of Joy

On the third day of Christmas, Jesus gave to me...
The Gift of Joy (the kind that laughs even when life gets heavy).

When Life Tries to Break You, Heaven Gives You a Reason to Smile Anyway

Joy is not a mood.

Joy is not a laugh.

Joy is not a "good day."

Joy is a supernatural rebellion. A holy refusal to let life decide how your spirit feels. A divine pushback against heaviness, sadness, drama, trauma, and everything that tried to make you fold. Joy is the gift Jesus gives you when life thinks it has you cornered.

Joy says,

"You may have hurt me... But you will NOT have my hope." "You may have shaken me... But you will NOT have my song." "You may have delayed me... But you will NOT have my destiny." Joy is heaven's reminder that you still belong to God even when the world tries to drain you. This is not regular joy. This is resurrection joy—the kind that gets up even when everything in your life says you shouldn't.

Joy That Breaks Through Darkness

Some people confuse joy with happiness. Happiness is cute... but happiness has conditions. Happiness depends on how your day went, who texted back, whether your bank account is smiling, whether your plans didn't fall apart, and whether everybody acted right. Happiness is moody. Happiness evaporates under pressure. Happiness needs everything to go right. But JOY? JOY is disrespectful. Joy will show up in a place where it has no business showing up. I've been at funerals where, in the middle of tears, a funny memory popped up, and suddenly the whole room was laughing. That wasn't disrespect—that was joy breaking the grip of death. Joy walks into the darkest rooms of your heart and flips on the lights like, "Alright, we're not doing this today." Joy grows in the soil of struggle. Joy blooms in the middle of disappointment. Joy sings in the valley. Joy dances in the fight. Joy refuses to leave, even when sadness sends eviction papers. This is why the Bible says, "The joy of the Lord is your strength." Not your smile. Not your money. Not your friends.

Not your circumstances. JOY is the strength. Joy is strength disguised as laughter.

The Joy Jesus Gives Does Not Need a Reason

Let me tell you the secret: Joy does not come FROM something. Joy comes WITH someone. You do not have joy because life is good—you have joy because Jesus is good. You do not have joy because everything is perfect—you have joy because His presence is perfect. Your circumstances may wobble. Your peace may be tested. Your heart may hurt. Your path may shift. But JOY stays because JESUS stays. Joy is not an emotion—It is evidence of His presence living inside you.

Joy That Refuses to Let Pain Have the Last Word

Joy is the spiritual reminder that your pain is NOT the end of your story.

The enemy will whisper, "You'll never get up again." Joy responds, "Watch me."

The enemy will whisper, "That broke you." Joy responds, "No... it BUILT me."

The enemy will whisper, "You won't smile again."

Joy responds, "Move back, I'm shining."

Joy does not deny pain—But it refuses to be defined by it.

Joy is the holy whisper that says,

"Your heart may be bruised... But it is still beating." "Your spirit may be tested... But it is still rising." "Your future may be unclear... But it is still unfolding." Joy is stubborn. Joy is defiant. Joy is spiritual resistance.

The Joy That Surprises You at the Most Unlikely Moments

Joy shows up like an unexpected Christmas gift—Right when you thought the season was too heavy, too cold, and too complicated.

Joy will ambush you in the middle of your:

Errands, prayers, quiet moments, heartbreak, memories, messy kitchen, lonely car ride, morning shower, late-night breakdown. Suddenly, something inside you warms up. Your spirit stretches. Your mind exhales. Your heart remembers it is still capable of gratitude.

Joy sneaks into your soul and whispers,

"You are still alive. You are still here. There is still a purpose for you. You still matter." Joy comes when you are not looking... because joy is not earned—It is given.

The Joy That Makes Your Enemies Confused

Let me get a little messy here—Joy will confuse the people waiting for you to fall apart. When they expect you to break, you get stronger. When they expect you to quit, you get bolder. When they expect you to disappear, you become more visible. When they expect you to snap, you walk in peace. Joy is the revenge you did not have to plan. Joy is the clapback without saying a word. Joy is the glow-up no one saw coming. Joy is the sign that God is still doing something inside you... Even when life tried to bury you outside.

Joy That Keeps You Moving Forward

Joy is momentum. Joy is motion. Joy is forward energy when everything tries to pull you backwards.

Joy says:

"You cannot stay stuck here." "You cannot quit here." "You cannot collapse here." "You cannot surrender here." Joy pushes your feet. Joy strengthens your spine. Joy sharpens your focus. Joy reminds you that better is still possible.

Joy says:

"I know it's been hard—but keep going." "I know it hurt—but keep living." "I know you're tired—but keep believing." Joy does not push you out of exhaustion—joy pulls you into purpose.

Your Christmas Joy Practice
A Daily Declaration

Find one thing today that makes you smile—a song, a memory, or even a funny video—and let yourself laugh. Then, look up and say, "Jesus, thank You for restoring my joy. This heavy season does not own me." Say it when you wake up. Say it when sadness taps your shoulder. Say it when fear whispers lies. Joy is not a feeling—it is a gift. And Jesus gives it freely.

This is Gift Number Three: The Gift of Joy.

Gift Number Four

The Gift of Love

On the fourth day of Christmas, Jesus gave to me...
The Gift of Love (the kind that sees my mess and chooses me anyway).

When God Loves You Past Your Fear, Your Failures, and the Foolishness You Don't Even Confess Out Loud

Love is not the warm, fuzzy thing you see on Christmas cards. It is not the Hallmark movie version where everybody apologizes in soft lighting. It is not the "bless your heart" love people give when they do not really mean it. The love Jesus gives you? Oh, that love is DIFFERENT. Holy different. Heavy difference. Life-altering. Different. It is the kind of love that walks into the room fully aware of your flaws, your fears, your secrets, your shame, and your messy moments and STILL says, "I choose you." And not just "I choose you when you behave." "I choose you when you pray enough." "I choose you when you get everything right." No—Jesus loves you with a no expiration date, no fine print, no return policy, and no seasonal availability kind of love.

This is Gift Number Four: the love that refuses to let you go.

The Love That Finds You Where You Hid

Let's be honest—humans hide. We hide behind confidence, busyness, success, humor, distractions, fake friendships, work, church activities, and "I'm fine" masks. We hide because we are afraid someone will see the part of us that is bleeding. I remember years ago, hiding behind a busy schedule because if I stopped moving, I'd have to feel how broken I really was. But Love found me in the busyness and said, "Be still." Jesus does not love the mask—He loves the YOU behind the mask. His love walks into the corners of your soul you have blocked off like a crime scene and whispers, "I am not scared of what you went through. And I am not leaving because of what you did." People love you until the truth shows up. Jesus loves you because the truth shows up. His love is not intimidated by your history. His love is not allergic to your mistakes. His love is not fragile. His love does not flinch. Jesus' love sees EVERYTHING... and still says, "This is my child."

Love That Covers Without Condemning

Some love exposes you. Some love embarrasses you. Some love keeps score. Some love says, "I'll forgive you, but I'll bring it up again next argument." But here is the good news: Jesus' love does not humiliate you—it heals you. He does not drag your past into every conversation. He does not weaponize your weakness. He does not replay your failures on a loop. His love covers WITHOUT condoning, corrects

WITHOUT crushing, and redeems WITHOUT rejecting. That is why Scripture says His love "covers a multitude of sins," Because His love is not invested in reminding you who you were—only in revealing who you can become.

Love That Rebuilds What Life Broke

Jesus' love is not sentimental—it is structural. His love becomes the scaffolding around your soul when life knocks down everything you built. His love rebuilds shattered confidence, wounded identity, broken trust, lost peace, unstable hope, and fractured self-worth. And the best part? Jesus does not rebuild you to who you were before. He rebuilds you BETTER. Stronger. Wiser. More compassionate. More grounded. More prepared. More YOU. His love strengthens what life weakened and upgrades what trauma downgraded. That is why the enemy fights your understanding of God's love—because once you know you are loved, you become impossible to manipulate.

Love That Does Not Wait For You to Deserve It

Human love usually comes with conditions. Earned. Negotiated. Performance-based. But Jesus gives love BEFORE transformation, not after. He does not say, "Fix yourself, then come to Me." He says, "Come to Me. I will fix you." He does not say, "Get it together, and then I'll love you." He says, "I love you now. I loved you then. I will love you forever." His love runs toward you, not away. His love picks you up when shame knocks you down. His love restores dignity to places where sin tried to erase it. His love says, "You are still worthy because I said so." This is the gift that unhooks you from perfectionism.

Love That Fights For Your Future

Let me tell you something true and tough: If Jesus did not love you, you would have stayed stuck. Stuck in patterns, addictions, cycles, toxic relationships, bad theology, fear, shame, and the version of yourself you outgrew. But His love fought for your evolution. His love disrupted your comfort zone. His love pushed you into healing. His love kept you alive when life tried to take you out. His love rescued dreams you thought were dead. His love whispered purpose into nights when you wanted to disappear. The reason you are still becoming... It is because His love would NOT let you settle for a lesser life.

Love That Teaches You How to Love Yourself

Now here comes the part we do not preach enough: You cannot love others well. And hate yourself quietly. Jesus' love becomes a mirror—but not the kind that shows your flaws. His love shows your value, your calling, your resilience, your sacredness, your identity, and your divine design. His love says, "You are Mine. And because you are Mine, you are enough." When you accept that love, you stop begging for attention, stop tolerating mistreatment, stop shrinking to make others comfortable, and stop apologizing for existing. Self-worth is not a luxury—it is the FRUIT of knowing God loves you.

Your Christmas Love Practice
December Declaration

Go to a mirror. Look at yourself—really look—and say this out loud to the person staring back: "Jesus loves you. He chose you. And He is not finished with you." Do this every day this season. Let His love sit with you. Let His love strengthen you. Let His love wash old lies off your spirit. Because Gift Number Four is not ordinary—it is the love that transforms everything it touches.

This is Gift Number Four: The Gift of Love.

Gift Number Five

The Gift of Grace

On the fifth day of Christmas, Jesus gave to me...
The Gift of Grace (to catch me when I trip and cover what I can't fix).

When You Run Out of Perfection, God Steps In

Grace is not a polite "excuse me." Grace is not just a prayer we say over a turkey that is a little too dry. Grace is the supernatural power that catches you when you trip, covers you when you fall, and kisses you on the forehead when you know—you KNOW—you messed up. Some gifts you earn. Some gifts you trade for. But Grace? Grace is the gift you get when you absolutely, positively do not deserve it. It is the unmerited, unearned, unexpected favor of God that steps in and says, "I know what the rules say, but I love this one too much to let them drown."

This is Gift Number Five—the gift that covers your past, handles your present, and secures your future.

The Grace That Catches You When You Trip

Let's be real. We all trip. We trip over our words. We trip over old habits. We trip over our temper. Especially in traffic or when that one relative starts talking politics at the dinner table. Religion tells you, "If you trip, you're out."

Grace tells you, "If you trip, I'll catch you."

Grace does not mean God ignores your mess. It means He refuses to let your mess define you. Grace is the reason you are still standing here today. It wasn't your alarm clock that woke you up—it was Grace. It wasn't your smarts that kept that job—it was Grace. It wasn't your patience that kept your family together—it was Grace (and maybe a little Jesus-juice in your coffee cup).

Grace For the People Who Get On Your Nerves

Now, here is the hard part. Jesus didn't just give you grace so you could feel good. He gave you grace so you could deal with THEM. You know who "them" is. The coworker who replies "Reply All" to every email. The family member who asks why you're still single. The person who cut you off on the highway. I admit, I have had moments in the grocery store line where I needed a "Grace transfusion" because the person in front of me had 40 items in the 10-items-or-less lane. But then I remember: God was patient with me when I had "40 items of sin" in His holy lane.

The Gift of Grace gives you the supernatural ability to look at them and say, "Lord, bless them... before I have to lay hands on them myself."

Grace is the buffer zone. It allows you to extend mercy to others because you remember how much mercy God extended to YOU. When you realize how much God has forgiven you, it gets a lot harder to hold a grudge against somebody else.

Grace That Silences the Accuser

The enemy loves to keep a record of your wrongs. He has a clipboard with every mistake you made since 1998. He whispers, "You call yourself a Christian? After what you did? After what you thought?" But Grace walks into the courtroom, takes the clipboard, rips it in half, and says, "Case dismissed." Grace does not just forgive—it forgets. It cleans the slate. It washes the stain. It removes the label. Grace says, "You are not your mistake. You are my miracle."

The Grace to Start Over... Right Now

You do not have to wait for New Year's Eve to start over. You do not have to wait for Monday. Grace is available at 2:00 PM on a Tuesday when you have just lost your temper. When you're crying in the bathroom at midnight, Grace is there to help. The Bible says His mercies are new EVERY morning. That means you get a fresh batch of Grace every single time the sun comes up. Did you mess up yesterday? Grace says, "Try again." Did you fail this morning? Grace says, "Get back up." Did you quit on your dream? Grace says, "Let's restart." Grace is the God of the Second Chance. And the third. And the fourth. And the four-hundredth.

The Grace That Is Sufficient

Paul (the apostle, not me—though I agree with him) begged God to take away a thorn in his flesh. He prayed three times. And God didn't fix it. God didn't remove it. God said, "My grace is sufficient for you." Translation: "I'm not going to make the problem go away, but I am going to make YOU strong enough to handle it." Sometimes the gift isn't the removal of the mountain. Sometimes the gift is the Grace to climb it. Grace empowers you to walk through seasons that would crush a normal person. Grace holds your head up high when shame tries to pull it down. Grace puts praise in your mouth when logic says you should be complaining.

Grace That Makes You Look Better Than You Are

Let's tell the truth. There are doors that opened for you that you did NOT have the key for. There are rooms you walked into that you were NOT qualified for. There are blessings that landed in your lap that you did NOT work for. That is the favor of Grace. Grace makes you look good. It puts God's glory on your life so that when people look at you, they don't see your struggle—they see His strength. They ask, "How did you do it?" And you just smile and point up. "I didn't. Grace did."

Your Christmas Grace Practice
A Daily Declaration

Identify one person who has annoyed you, hurt you, or frustrated you this week. (It might even be yourself). Now, say this: "I release them to God. I extend the same Grace to them that Jesus extended to me." Do it before you drink your coffee. Clear the air so you can breathe. You are not perfect. But because of Grace, you are perfectly loved.

This is Gift Number Five: The Gift of Grace.

Gift Number Six
TheGift of Courage

On the sixth day of Christmas, Jesus gave to me...
The Gift of Courage (to walk into rooms my fear told me to avoid).

The Strength to Walk Into What You've Been Afraid to Even Pray For

Courage is not the absence of fear—it is the divine audacity to move while your legs are still shaking. Courage is the gift Jesus slides into your spirit when life has bullied you long enough, when fear has held your future hostage, when your purpose is suffocated by hesitation, and when you have been overthinking more than you have been obeying.

Courage says, "I may be scared... but I am still going."

If fear is the prison, courage is the key.

This is Gift Number Six—the one that pushes you, pulls you, lifts you, and dares you to stop living small.

Courage Is Not Bravery—It Is Obedience

People think courage is having no fear. Wrong.

Courage means:

fear showed up, fear spoke up, fear tried to take the mic, fear tried to run the meeting, fear tried to talk you OUT of yourself, and you replied, "Yeah, I hear you... But I am doing it anyway." Courage is not loud. Courage is not showy. Courage is not always visible. Sometimes courage looks like sending an email that scares you, trying again after failing, saying "no" when you are used to saying "yes," walking away from what is unhealthy, applying for the job, releasing the book, releasing the grudge, showing up when you feel insecure, and believing God still has plans for you. Obedience creates courage. When you move with God, fear loses its power.

The Courage Jesus Gives Will Rearrange Your Entire Life

Here is the truth we do not preach enough: when Jesus gives you courage, He does not give you permission—He gives you assignments.

Courage says:

"You can step into rooms your insecurity told you were off-limits." "You can heal from trauma that tried to be your permanent roommate." "You can embrace opportunities that terrify you." "You can confront what has controlled you." "You can become someone your past cannot recognize."

Courage is the spiritual shove you need when your destiny has been standing there tapping its foot like, "Well? Are we going or not?"

Courage Is Born in the Very Place That Broke You

Let me get real: Courage rarely begins on the mountaintop.

Courage is born in:

The valley, the heartbreak, the betrayal, the waiting room, the lonely season, the doctor's office, the prayer you prayed through tears, the night you questioned everything, the moment you felt small. Courage comes from the places where you thought you would never get up again. I know what it's like to have the wind knocked out of you by life, to sit on the edge of the bed and wonder if you have the strength to put your socks on. But that very moment of weakness is where God starts building your steel. Jesus does not give you courage OUTSIDE your wounds—He shapes it WITHIN them. Your courage is not random—it is manufactured from your survival. That is why your courage is dangerous—because it comes with receipts.

Courage That Talks Back to Fear

Fear is loud. Fear loves drama. Fear loves to narrate every worst-case scenario like it is auditioning for a horror movie. Fear says, "You are not ready." "You will embarrass yourself." "What if they reject you?" "What if you fail?" "What if you succeed—then they expect too much?" "What if your past shows up?" But courage responds, "And what if God shows up?" "What if this time is different?" "What if my obedience changes everything?" "What if my healing scares the devil?" "What if my calling finds me once I move?" Fear asks questions to trap you. Courage asks questions to free you.

Courage to Become the Version of You Heaven Sees

Let me say something that might sting but will save your life: You are not afraid of failure—you are afraid of becoming the person God designed you to be. Because that version is confident, is disciplined, is powerful, is healed, is visible, is bold, is focused, is unstoppable, and THAT version terrifies fear itself. Jesus gives you courage not just to face life, but to face YOU.

Courage says, "I am no longer shrinking to fit who I used to be." Courage That Walks You Into Rooms You Prayed For

God's courage will make you walk into opportunity while still sweating, sit at tables you never thought you deserved, speak up when your voice trembles, pivot directions when He says move, stand tall when people hope you crumble, and show up in arenas where no one expects you.

Courage does not ask, "Do you feel ready?"

Courage asks, "Are you willing?"

If you say yes, courage says, "Alright then—let's go."

Courage Is the Thing the Enemy Did Not Want You to Have

Fear knew that once you grabbed courage, generational cycles would shatter, depression would lose its grip, boldness would rise, your voice would return, your gifts would activate, your destiny would unlock, your identity would strengthen, and your purpose would roar. Fear's biggest nightmare is you becoming fearless. Because nothing scares you—but because nothing stops you. Courage does not eliminate fear. Courage DEMOTES fear.

Your Christmas Courage Practice
A December Declaration

Identify one thing you have been avoiding out of fear. A conversation? A decision? An application? A prayer? Do it today. Even if you do it shaking. Then say, "Jesus, I am moving because You are with me." Courage is not a personality trait—it is a spiritual gift. And Jesus wrapped it with your name on it.

This is Gift Number Six: The Gift of Courage.

Gift Number Seven
The Gift of Identity

On the seventh day of Christmas, Jesus gave to me...
The Gift of Identity (reminding me who I was before the world labeled me).

When Jesus Hands You Back the You That Life Tried to Steal

Identity is not who you see in the mirror. Identity is not who people say you are. Identity is not what your family expected. Identity is not the nickname somebody gave you at 12 that you are still carrying around in your spirit like it is part of your DNA. Identity is the unshakeable truth heaven spoke over you before earth ever labeled you.

Identity is the core of who you are when you strip away:

Titles trauma performances coping mechanisms masks roles survival tactics people-pleasing "I'm fine" lies childhood wounds grown-up scars Identity is the YOU God designed before life tried to redesign you.

This is Gift Number Seven—the gift that reminds you of your original blueprint.

The Day You Were Born, Purpose Was Released Into the Earth

Your identity didn't start when you took your first breath. Identity began when God said, "Let there be YOU." Before the doctor heard your cry, heaven heard your calling. You were not an accident. You were not an afterthought. You were not a surprise. You were not a mistake wrapped in a human body. You were a divine assignment sent into the world with a specific sound, a specific light, a specific footprint, a specific anointing, a specific mission, and a specific GIFT that only YOU could carry. When Jesus restores your identity, He is peeling back every layer that life piled on top of your purpose.

The Identity Jesus Gives Is Not Fragile

Human identity is fragile. If people approve of you, you feel worthy. If they criticize you, you fall apart. If they clap, you rise. If they ignore you, you shrink. But the identity Jesus gives? Ohhhh, it is BUILT FOR WAR. This identity survives heartbreak, outlives betrayal, heals from rejection, grows through trauma, outsmarts insecurity, silences shame, resurrects self-worth, and outlasts every storm your life did not order. Your God-given identity cannot be stolen—only forgotten. Fear blurred it. People distorted it. Life distracted you. Trauma tried to bury it. But Jesus says, "Let Me remind you who you are."

Identity That Breaks the Hold of Other People's Opinions

Let's go ahead and snatch the band-aid off: Most of your stress has come from letting people who were not qualified to name you define you. Somebody's insecurity shaped your self-esteem. Somebody's fear shaped your decisions. Somebody's jealousy shaped your confidence. Somebody's ignorance shaped your potential. Somebody's rejection shaped your worth. Jesus looks at all of that and says, "Give me that. It is not yours anymore." When Jesus restores identity, you stop auditioning for acceptance. You stop begging for validation. You stop shrinking to make others comfortable. You stop performing to keep the peace.

Identity says, "I know who I am—and I will not negotiate my value." Identity That Survives What Should Have Destroyed You

Let me tell you something real: There were moments in your life that should have swallowed you whole. Moments that should have shredded your identity until nothing was left but pieces. But identity holds memory. Spiritual memory. Divine memory. The reason you are still standing is that your identity refused to die in the dark. Your identity remembered God's promise when your mind forgot. Your identity remembered purpose when your heart was broken. Your identity remembered strength when your spirit was trembling.

Identity whispered, "You are still chosen. You are still called. You are still needed. You are still destined."

Identity is your spiritual backbone.

Identity That Frees You From Who You Used to Be

Some people are in love with your old version. They fell in love with your brokenness because it made them feel big. They fell in love with your silence because it kept them comfortable. They fell in love with your insecurity because it kept you predictable. They fell in love with your trauma because they could control you through it. But identity says, "I am not who I was. I am not who they want me to be. I am becoming who God always saw." Identity is liberation. Identity is spiritual emancipation. Identity is the end of apologizing for evolving. If they cannot handle your growth, they can watch from a distance.

Identity That Positions You For Destiny

Here's the truth: Destiny is reserved for people who know who they are. When you embrace your identity, doors open. Assignments activate. Connections align. Favor follows. Clarity strengthens. Purpose intensifies. Identity is not just spiritual—it is strategic. God cannot bless the version of you that is hiding behind fear. He blesses the REAL you. The CALLED you. The CHOSEN you. The YOU He handcrafted in eternity. Identity positions you to receive what you were always meant to carry.

Your Christmas Identity Practice
A Declaration For December

Take a piece of paper. On one side, write down the labels people have given you (Too loud, Too sensitive, Not enough, Damaged). Now, rip that paper in half. Throw it away. Then, say this: "I am who GOD says I am. I am chosen. I am loved. I am His." Because Gift Number Seven is not about who you became—it is about who you ALWAYS WERE.

This is Gift Number Seven: The Gift of Identity.

Gift Number Eight
The Gift of Revelation

On the eighth day of Christmas, Jesus gave to me...
The Gift of Revelation (so I can finally see what I've been missing).

When Jesus Open Your Eyes **to What Has Been Right In Front of You the Entire Time**

Revelation is not information. Revelation is not knowledge. Revelation is not "fun facts about the Bible."

Revelation is when heaven pulls back the curtain and lets you SEE. SEE truth. SEE purpose. SEE patterns. SEE people. SEE direction. SEE danger. SEE opportunity. SEE YOURSELF.

Revelation is heaven whispering, "Look again—you missed something."

It is the moment God says, "You thought you knew what was going on... but let Me show you what's REALLY happening."

This is Gift Number Eight—the ability to SEE what others overlook.

Revelation Is a Light Switch In a Dark Room

Life will have you walking through seasons so dark you bump into things that do not even belong to you. You stumble over old fears, inherited beliefs, misunderstandings, misaligned relationships, emotional blind spots, spiritual traps, and self-sabotage. But Revelation walks into the room and flips the switch. Suddenly you can SEE: "Oh, that wasn't rejection—that was protection." "Oh, that wasn't a setback—that was a setup." "Oh, that wasn't punishment—that was preparation." "Oh, that wasn't betrayal—that was direction." "Oh, that wasn't confusion—that was calling." Revelation will embarrass your old interpretation of life and elevate your understanding to the level of heaven.

Revelation Saves You Years of Heartache

Let's tell the truth: Some of our wounds came from what we refused to see. We ignored the signs. We romanticized the red flags. We excused behavior because we did not want to deal with the truth. We stayed in rooms that were draining us. We trusted voices we should have muted. We carried responsibilities that never belonged to us. But revelation interrupts the cycle. Revelation says, "You cannot fix what you will not FACE." Revelation is not always comfortable—but it is always necessary. God loves you too much to let you stay blind.

Revelation Teaches You How to Discern, Not Just React

Without revelation, you overthink, you misjudge, you jump to conclusions, you try to fix what is not yours, you fight battles that are beneath you, you misinterpret silence, you over-invest in the wrong places, and you under-invest in the right ones. But when Jesus gives you revelation, your reactions slow down because your discernment speeds up. Revelation shifts your decision-making from emotional to spiritual. Revelation upgrades your instincts. You stop responding from fear and start responding from wisdom. You stop chasing answers and start noticing patterns. You stop falling for potential and start reading fruit.

Revelation Will Change How You See Yourself

You think you know yourself? Baby, wait until God reveals you... to YOU.

Revelation helps you see:

Strengths you downplayed, gifts you ignored, wounds you never acknowledged, callings you ran from, authority you forgot, resilience you underestimated, purpose you buried under stress

Revelation is God saying, "Look again. You are more powerful than you realize."

Sometimes the biggest mystery in your life is you. And revelation solves it.

Revelation Exposes What the Enemy Hoped You Would Never Notice

Let me talk real: The enemy does not fear your praise—he fears your perception. Because once you SEE, you stop falling for traps that used to trip you. You stop returning to cycles that used to enslave you. You stop believing lies that used to weaken you. You stop letting the wrong people speak into your life. You stop surrendering your peace to situations beneath your anointing. The enemy's power depends on your blindness. Revelation ends that contract. Once God makes it clear, you cannot unsee it. And that clarity becomes your freedom.

Revelation Is the Birthplace of Transformation

Change does not start with action—it starts with clarity. You cannot heal what you cannot see. You cannot grow from what you cannot identify. You cannot break what you cannot acknowledge. You cannot pursue what you cannot recognize. Revelation gives you the blueprint.

Revelation is the moment your mind wakes up, and your spirit says:

"Oh... THAT is why God allowed this season." "Oh... THAT is the direction I need to move." "Oh... THAT is the habit I need to break." "Oh... THAT is the conversation I need to have." "Oh... THAT is the mindset blocking my progress." Revelation is not random—it is a divine strategy.

Your Christmas Revelation Practice
A December Declaration

Sit quietly for five minutes today. Ask God this one question: "Lord, show me what I am missing." Then, listen. Don't talk. Just look and listen. Say, "Jesus, open my eyes to what I have ignored, misunderstood, or mislabeled." Revelation is not just a moment—it is a lifestyle.

This is Gift Number Eight: The Gift of Revelation.

Gift Number Nine
The Gift of Strength

On the ninth day of Christmas, Jesus gave to me...
The Gift of Strength (to keep standing when I wanted to quit).

When Jesus Gives You the Power to Stand In Places You Should Have Fallen

Strength is not flexing muscles. Strength is not "I'm good" while you're falling apart. Strength is not pretending life didn't hit you. Strength is the supernatural ability to keep moving when your heart is tired, your mind is overwhelmed, your soul is aching, and everything around you whispers, "Sit this one out."

Strength is the evidence that God stepped into your weakness and said, "I will carry you through this."

This is Gift Number Nine—the strength that is not human... but holy.

Strength Is Not How Loud You Roar—It Is How Long You Endure

People misunderstand strength. They think it is being tough, acting unbothered, pretending nothing hurts, never breaking down, and keeping a hard shell. FALSE. Strength is endurance. Strength is resilience. Strength is the refusal to quit. Strength is the ability to take a hit, wobble, cry, pray, exhale—and STILL stand. Strength is the grace to stay in the ring long after fear told you to forfeit. When God strengthens you, He builds something in you that life cannot bend.

The Strength Jesus Gives Shows Up When Yours Is Gone

Ohhh, let's get real right here—there were moments when your courage ran out, your joy ran thin, your hope was on life support, your patience expired, your faith was flickering like a dying bulb, and you said to yourself, "I cannot take one more thing." But somehow... SOMEHOW... you kept going. That was not you. That was God strengthening you. That strength was not natural—it was supernatural. It was heaven whispering, "I am lending you My strength for this season." God's strength is the reason your breakdown did not break you down.

Strength Is Born in the Places You Once Feared

Strength does not grow on mountaintops. Strength is forged in fire. Strength matures in storms. Strength develops under pressure. Your strength came from what hurt you, what stretched you, what scared you, what humbled you, what disappointed you, what you survived secretly, what you outgrew quietly, what you overcame silently, and what you endured when no one checked on you. The very place you cried in became the place God strengthened you. Your tears watered your strength. Your pain matured your strength. Your past activated your strength. Strength comes from survival.

Strength That Tells the Enemy "Not Today."

Let me talk boldly: Sometimes the enemy does not need you to fall—he just needs you to quit. He whispers, "You're too tired." "You're too old." "You're too broken." "You're too late." "You're too messed up." "You're too behind." But the strength Jesus gives you responds, "You might be right—but I'm STILL going."

Strength tells fear, "You can ride in the car, but you cannot drive."

Strength tells doubt, "You can knock, but you cannot enter." Strength tells trials, "You can show up, but you cannot win."

That is holy strength. Defiant strength. Strength that stands even when shaking.

Strength That Looks Normal On the Outside But Is Miraculous On the Inside

People watch you and say, "How did you get through that?" "How are you still smiling?" "How are you still working?" "How are you still dreaming?" "How are you not bitter?" "How did you not lose your mind?" And you could explain it... But honestly? They would not understand. Because they are seeing the OUTSIDE of you—but God strengthened the INSIDE of you.

Strength is invisible until life pulls on it. Then suddenly it shows up like a soldier stepping out of the shadows, saying:

"I've been here the whole time."

Strength That Lets You Rest Without Quitting

Strength is not pushing 24/7. Strength is knowing when to stop and breathe. Rest is not weakness. Rest is part of strength. Jesus gives you strength that lets you sit down without collapsing, pause without panicking, breathe without guilt, and rest knowing the world will NOT fall apart just because you took a break. Strength knows when to fight—and when to recharge. Strength knows when to speak—and when to be silent.

Strength knows when to move—and when God is saying, "Be still. I'm handling this."

Your Christmas Strength Practice
A December Declaration

Identify the one area in your life where you feel ready to quit. Is it your marriage? Your job? Your healing? Lay your hand on that area (or on your heart) and say, "Lord, I am weak here. Be my strength. I trade my exhaustion for Your power." Strength is not something you earn—it is something God GIVES. And He gives it freely.

This is Gift Number Nine: The Gift of Strength.

Gift Number Ten

The Gift of Purpose

On the tenth day of Christmas, Jesus gave to me...The Gift of Purpose (because I'm not just surviving, I'm on assignment).

When Jesus Hands You the Blueprint For Why You Are Still Here

Purpose is not your job. Purpose is not your title. Purpose is not your degree. Purpose is not your resume. Purpose is not your platform. Purpose is the divine WHY behind your existence.

Purpose is the gravitational pull on your soul that refuses to let you quit, even when everything in your life says, "Just stop."

Purpose is the supernatural reminder that "You were born ON assignment."

This is Gift Number Ten—the gift that explains your survival.

Purpose Is the Reason the Attacks Didn't Work

Somebody needs to shout right here: The reason the enemy fought you THIS hard is because of what you are carrying. Purpose is the threat. Fear is a distraction. Depression is a distraction. Confusion is a distraction. People's opinions are distractions. Setbacks are distractions. The attacks were NEVER about your past—they were always about your FUTURE. Purpose puts a target on your back, but it also puts POWER in your spirit. You are not still here because you got lucky. You are here because your purpose refused to die.

Purpose is the Internal GPS That Won't Let You Get Lost

Purpose will look you dead in the face and say:

"Nope. Wrong turn. Fix it." "Nope. You're out of alignment; come back." "Nope. You're settling; get up." "Nope. You're grieving too long; breathe." "Nope. That relationship is draining you; unplug." "Nope. That opportunity is beneath your calling." Purpose is brutally honest because destiny is too important to sugarcoat. Purpose will drag you out of rooms you were never meant to sit in and shove you into growth you tried to avoid. And YES—it may frustrate you. But it will NEVER fail you.

Purpose Is Born in Pain, Not Comfort

We do not like this part... but it is the truth. Your purpose is connected to the places that hurt the most. Your pain shaped your compassion. Your trauma sharpened your discernment. Your storms built your endurance. Your heartbreak birthed your wisdom. Your failures developed your humility. Your losses deepened your empathy. Purpose is NEVER born in comfort—comfort cannot produce transformation. Your pain may have been your greatest teacher, but your purpose is your greatest assignment.

Purpose Is God Saying, "You Are Necessary."

You are not random. You are not replaceable. You are not optional. You are not accidental. You are NECESSARY. Your voice is necessary. Your story is necessary. Your creativity is necessary. Your survival is necessary. Your healing is necessary. Your testimony is necessary. Your perspective is necessary. Your light is necessary.

Purpose says, "You matter to the world in ways you haven't even discovered yet."

Purpose makes you valuable beyond applause. Purpose gives you meaning beyond validation. Purpose makes you powerful beyond people's approval.

Purpose Makes Your Feet Move Even When Your Heart Hesitates. Purpose grabs you by the collar and says:

"I know you're scared—move anyway." "I know you're tired—keep going." "I know you're confused—trust Me." "I know you've never done this—go forward." "I know your past is loud—walk louder." Purpose will have you doing things you NEVER imagined you could do. Purpose pushes you into places your insecurity tried to block. Purpose activates gifts you forgot you had. Purpose forces you to grow into the version of you that heaven sees. Purpose is not gentle. Purpose is not weak. Purpose is not soft. Purpose is POWERFUL.

Purpose Reveals Why You Had to Survive What You Did

There were things that almost broke you... But now you see they BUILT you. There were seasons that crushed you... But now they CROWN you. There were tears that drowned you... But now they WATER your purpose. There were nights you thought you'd never recover from... But now those nights are part of your testimony. Purpose helps you reinterpret your entire life. You stop saying, "Why me?" And start saying, "Thank You for trusting me with this assignment." Your pain was not punishment—it was preparation.

Purpose Is the Reason You Can't Fit In Anywhere. You Don't Belong

Purpose makes you allergic to mediocrity. Purpose makes you uncomfortable in small spaces. Purpose makes you restless around the wrong people. Purpose makes you irritated with distractions. Purpose makes you outgrow things QUICK. Purpose refuses to let you shrink into a version of yourself that dishonors your destiny.

Purpose says, "You weren't built for normal—you were built for divine impact."

Your Christmas Purpose Practice
A December Declaration

Write this on a sticky note and put it on your bathroom mirror: "I am not an accident. I am an assignment." Read it every morning. Then pray: "Jesus, reveal the purpose behind my survival and give me the courage to walk in it." Purpose is not a journey you create—it is a plan God already wrote. Your job is to walk into it.

This is Gift Number Ten: The Gift of Purpose.

Gift Number Eleven

The Gift of Hope

On the eleventh day of Christmas, Jesus gave to me...
The Gift of Hope (the anchor that holds when everything else lets go).

When Jesus Hands You the One Thing That Refuses to Die Even When Everything Else Does

Hope is not optimism. Hope is not "positive thinking." Hope is not pretending things are better than they are. Hope is a spiritual anchor. Hope is a lifeline. Hope is the whisper that shows up at the very moment you think you've taken your last breath emotionally.

Hope says:

"This is NOT the end. You STILL have a future. You STILL have purpose. You STILL have God. You STILL have breath. You STILL have a breakthrough being prepared with your name on it." Hope is stubborn. Hope is relentless. Hope is the most disrespectful gift God gave to your darkness—because it REFUSES to leave.

This is Gift Number Eleven—the gift that holds you together while heaven rebuilds you.

Hope Shows Up When Everything Else Walks Away

Let's be honest: People leave. Confidence leaves. Energy leaves. Peace leaves. Excitement leaves. Motivation leaves. Opportunities leave. But HOPE?

Hope walks in like, "Yeah, I heard everything fell apart—move, let me sit down."

Hope is the friend that does not need your situation to improve before it commits to your story.

Hope sits in the ashes with you and still says, "You're getting up from this."

Hope believes in you when you can't believe in yourself.

Hope Is a Fighter—Not a Feeling

Hope doesn't just comfort—it CONFRONTS. Hope confronts depression. Hope confronts anxiety. Hope confronts discouragement. Hope confronts unbelief. Hope confronts every voice telling you to quit. Hope fights your darkness with the memory of God's faithfulness.

Hope drags your weary soul by the hand and says, "I know you're tired—but your story is not done."

Hope is holy resistance.

Hope Reminds You That God Is Still Writing

One of the most painful human experiences is feeling like your story is finished before your miracle shows up. But hope whispers, "Turn the page." Because every single time life tried to end your chapter, God said, "No, we're not done here."

Hope is the spiritual reminder that:

God still has a plan, God still has a timeline, God still has an answer, God still has a healing, God still has a breakthrough, God still has a purpose, God still has a promise

Hope says, "Your current chapter is NOT your final chapter." Hope Survives Where Faith Feels Fragile

Some days your faith is strong. Some days your faith is shaky. Some days, your faith whispers, "Lord, I believe... help my unbelief." But hope? Hope steps in when faith is flickering.

Hope says, "Even if you can't see the miracle yet, keep breathing—it's coming."

Hope does not replace faith—it REINFORCES it. Hope holds you steady until faith strengthens again. Hope is the safety net for your soul.

Hope Is Why Your Heart Didn't Stay Broken

You've been through things that should have left you emotionally paralyzed. But somewhere inside you—even when you didn't feel spiritual, even when you weren't praying right, even when you weren't strong, even when you thought God was quiet—HOPE kept beating.

Hope said:

"You can cry, but you cannot collapse." "You can grieve, but you cannot give up." "You can hurt, but you cannot lose yourself." "You can lose some things, but you will NOT lose your future." Hope stitched your heart together while you slept. Hope protected you while you healed. Hope refuses to let the enemy write your ending.

Hope Is a Holy Preview of What God Is About to Do

Hope is not about what you SEE—it's about what you SENSE.

Hope gives you glimpses of:

New beginnings, answered prayers, future favor, divine connections, restored relationships, financial breakthroughs, mental healing, spiritual elevation, and personal transformation. Hope is a sacred preview, a prophetic trailer for a movie God is about to release in your life.

Hope tells your spirit, "SOMETHING is coming—and it is GOOD." Hope Makes You Dangerous to the Devil

The enemy can handle you being sad. He can handle you being tired. He can handle you being discouraged. But HOPE? Hope messes up his entire strategy. A hopeful believer is one who refuses to stay defeated.

Hope says:

"Even if life knocked me down—I'm getting back up again." "Even if the storm hit me hard—my story is not over." "Even if this season was rough—my next one is redeemed." Hope makes you emotionally, spiritually, and mentally RESILIENT. Hope is the comeback energy of heaven.

Your Christmas Hope Practice
A December Declaration

Close your eyes. Imagine yourself one year from now—healed, whole, and smiling. Hold that picture in your mind. That is your prophecy. Now say, "Jesus, restore my hope. I believe my future is bright because You are already there." Hope is not just a feeling—hope is a lifeline.

This is Gift Number Eleven: The Gift of Hope.

Gift Number Twelve
The Gift of Salvation

On the twelfth day of Christmas, Jesus gave to me...
The Gift of Salvation (The greatest trade: my brokenness for His life).

When Jesus Gives You the One Gift That Can Rebuild, Redefine, Restore, and Rescue Your Entire Life

Salvation is not a church membership. Salvation is not a moment at the altar. Salvation is not a "get out of hell free" card. Salvation is not a spiritual badge you earn for behaving. Salvation is the deepest love letter heaven ever wrote, signed in blood, delivered in grace, sealed by mercy, and handed to you with open arms, saying, "Come home. I want you." Salvation is God refusing to let your story end in darkness. Salvation is heaven, throwing you a lifeline when you didn't even know you were drowning. Salvation is the ultimate gift — the gift that gives ALL the other gifts power.

Salvation Is God Saying, "I Want You As You Are."

Most people think salvation requires perfection. But salvation is the OPPOSITE of perfection.

Salvation says:

"I want you BROKEN. I want you CONFUSED. I want you TIRED. I want you CRYING. I want you SHAKING. I want you AS YOU ARE—and together, we will build the person you are becoming." Jesus does not wait for you to get your life together. He steps INTO your mess and says, "Let's start here." Salvation is God meeting you at the bottom and lifting you into the life you never knew you deserved.

Salvation is the Beautiful Exchange. Salvation is a trade heaven initiates:

You bring your sin, your shame, your guilt, your regret, your trauma, your burdens, your fear, your mistakes, your past, And Jesus gives you: grace mercy forgiveness, identity restoration healing purpose freedom NEW LIFE Salvation is the most UNFAIR trade in history—and somehow, Jesus insists you walk away with the better end of the deal.

Salvation Breaks Every Chain You Think You Deserve to Keep

Some of the chains holding you were not placed by demons — they were placed by guilt. "I messed up too much." "I knew better." "I failed again." "I disappointed God." "I ruined everything." "I don't deserve a second chance."

Salvation steps in and says, "WATCH ME."

Salvation breaks chains you thought were welded. Salvation erases stains you thought were permanent. Salvation frees you from prisons you built yourself. This gift does not just open doors—it opens hearts.

Salvation Is Heaven's Proof That You Still Have a Future

When you accepted Jesus, heaven threw a celebration bigger than any Christmas party you've ever seen. Because salvation is: A new beginning A new identity A new destiny A new lineage A new legacy A new covenant

 A new life

Salvation is heaven declaring, "You have a FUTURE, and it is GOOD."

Life may have broken you, but salvation restores you. The enemy may have lied to you, but salvation reminds you who you are. Your past may have shamed you, but salvation rewrites your ending.

Salvation Makes You Dangerous

Let me tell you the truth with some Holy Ghost seasoning: Hell does NOT fear your talent. Hell does NOT fear your connections. Hell does NOT fear your money. Hell does NOT fear your personality.

Hell fears your salvation. Because salvation gives you authority, gives you access, gives you power, gives you discernment, gives you spiritual backing, gives you divine protection, and gives you Kingdom identity. Once you know who you are in Christ, every lie loses power. Every attack loses force. Every fear loses confidence. Salvation makes you spiritually UNTOUCHABLE.

Salvation Is the Gift You Grow Into Every Day

Salvation is not a moment—it is a journey. Every day, salvation teaches you something new: How to forgive. How to trust. How to pray. How to heal. How to grow. How to let go. How to rise again. How to walk in purpose. How to silence shame. How to hear God's voice. Salvation is a relationship—not a ritual. The more you walk with Jesus, the more salvation unfolds inside you.

Salvation Is the Greatest Gift Because It Makes Every Other Gift Possible

Without salvation, joy is temporary. Peace is unpredictable. Strength is inconsistent. Identity is shaky. The purpose is confusing. Hope is fragile. But WITH salvation? EVERY other gift becomes permanent, powerful, and unstoppable. Salvation is the foundation beneath every miracle God is preparing for you. Salvation is the reason your story continues. Salvation is the reason your destiny is guaranteed. Salvation is the reason your name is written in heaven. Salvation is the reason death cannot defeat you. Salvation is EVERYTHING.

Your Christmas Salvation Practice
A December Declaration

If you have never said yes to Jesus, say it now. If you have, say yes to Him again in a fresh way. Then declare, "Jesus, thank You for saving me. I trade my brokenness for Your life. I am Yours." Say it with gratitude. Say it with awe. Say it with joy. Say it with reverence. Say it with expectation. You are saved. You are covered. You are redeemed. You are chosen. You are God's.

This is Gift Number Twelve: The Gift of Salvation.

Conclusion
The Gifts Keep Giving

I want you to understand loudly, clearly, and without apology: these twelve gifts did not originate from me. I was never the source. I was only the carrier. They came *through* me, shaped by story, scar, and survival, and they were wrapped in love with **your name already on them**. Nothing in these pages was accidental. If something landed heavy, or gentle, or right on time, that was not coincidence. That was the intention.

Grace is for you—when you feel worthy and when you do not. Mercy is for you—especially on the days you replay what you wish you had done differently. Joy is for you, not the loud kind you perform, but the quiet kind that steadies you when life gets noisy. Peace is for you, even when your world refuses to calm down. Identity is for you, because you are more than what happened to you. Purpose is for you, even if you are still discovering it one step at a time. Strength is for you when you are tired of being strong. Revelation is for you when answers unfold slowly. Salvation is for you—complete, secure, and not dependent on your perfection.

These gifts are not seasonal. They do not fade when the lights come down or the calendar turns. They do not expire on December 26. You cannot outgrow them, outrun them, or out-sin them. They do not get revoked because you struggled, doubted, paused, or fell. They are not rewards for good behavior; they are evidence of love that does not quit.

This Christmas may come and go—but **the Giver stays**. When the wrapping paper is gone, when the music quiets, when real life shows back up at your door, He is still there. Walking with you. Covering you. Holding you steady.

So hold these gifts close. Use them daily. Return to them as naturally as you breathe. Come back to grace. Lean into mercy. Stand in your identity. Rest in peace. Walk in purpose. Draw from strength. Stay open to revelation. Trust salvation. Because Jesus did not give you these gifts for a moment, a season, or a holiday.

He gave them to you **for a lifetime**.

Afterword

A Christmas That Changed Me Too

I didn't just write these gifts... I lived them.

There were moments I didn't think I'd finish this book. Moments, I doubted myself. Moments life hit me hard enough to knock the creativity clean out of my spirit. Moments, I needed these gifts as much as anybody reading.

But every time I wanted to put down the pen, God said, "Paul... somebody needs this." So thank you—for being the reason I kept going.

As you unwrap these gifts, remember that Jesus is unwrapping YOU. Your healing. Your calling. Your future. Your identity. Your purpose.

This book changed me while I wrote it. I pray it changes you while you read it.

Reflection Questions

For Your Heart, Not Just Your Mind

See these questions slowly. Let them marinate. Let them work on you. Healing comes in waves—don't rush it.

1. Which gift spoke to you the loudest—and why?

2. Where in your life do you feel Jesus inviting you to grow next?

3. Which gift have you been afraid to receive?

4. How has your understanding of Jesus changed after reading this?

5. What old belief about yourself do you feel God breaking?

6. Where do you need grace most right now?

7. Who in your life needs one of these gifts shared with them?

8. What gift will you practice daily over the next 12 days?

9. Which chapter felt like Jesus was talking directly to you?

10. What will you do differently after finishing this book?

A Final Note To My Readers

Thank You For Sitting With Me

If you made it this far, thank you for sitting with me. Not skimming, not rushing, not trying to fix what you read—just staying. This book asked you to slow down, to feel some things that might have felt familiar, uncomfortable, or close to home. And instead of closing it early, you stayed in the room with me. That matters.

Some pages were not written to be impressive. They were written to be honest. I did not need applause or agreement—I needed witnesses. And by reading, by holding these words without judgment, you did exactly that. You did not interrupt the story. You did not tell me how it should have ended. You simply allowed it to be what it was. That kind of reading is a quiet kind of love, and I do not take it lightly.

So thank you for your time, your attention, and your willingness to sit with someone else's truth long enough to hear your own breathing in it. When you closed this book, I hope you did not feel like you finished something—but like you were accompanied through it. If nothing else, I hope you felt less alone. Because writing it reminded me that I was not either.

Thank you for sitting with me.